FESTIVE FOODS
MEXICO

Sylvia Goulding

CHELSEA
CLUBHOUSE

An Imprint of Chelsea House Publishers

Chelsea Clubhouse
An imprint of Chelsea House Publishers
132 West 31st Street
New York, NY 10001

Library of Congress Cataloging-in-Publication Data

Goulding, Sylvia.
  Festive foods / Sylvia Goulding. – 1st ed.
    v. cm.
  Includes bibliographical references and index.
  Contents: [1] China – [2] France – [3] Germany – [4] India – [5] Italy – [6] Japan – [7] Mexico – [8] United States.
  ISBN 978-0-7910-9751-9 (v. 1) – ISBN 978-0-7910-9752-6 (v. 2) – ISBN 978-0-7910-9756-4 (v. 3) – ISBN 978-0-7910-9757-1 (v. 4) – ISBN 978-0-7910-9753-3 (v. 5) – ISBN 978-0-7910-9754-0 (v. 6) – ISBN 978-0-7910-9755-7 (v. 7) – ISBN 978-0-7910-9758-8 (v. 8)
  1. Cookery, International. 2. Gardening. 3. Manners and customs. I. Title.
  TX725.A1G56 2008
  641.59–dc22

                    2007042722

Chelsea Clubhouse books are available at special discounts when purchased in bulk quantities for businesses, associations, institutions, or sales promotions. Please call our Special Sales Department in New York at (212) 967-8800 or (800) 322-8755.

You can find Chelsea Clubhouse
on the World Wide Web at
http://www.chelseahouse.com

Printed and bound in Dubai

10 9 8 7 6 5 4 3 2 1

For The Brown Reference Group plc.:
Project Editor: Sylvia Goulding
Cooking Editor: Angelika Ilies
Contributors: Jacqueline Fortey, Sylvia Goulding
Photographers: Klaus Arras, Emanuelle Morgan
Cartographer: Darren Awuah
Art Editor: Paula Keogh
Illustrator: Jo Gracie
Picture Researcher: Mike Goulding
Managing Editor: Bridget Giles
Production Director: Alastair Gourlay
Editorial Director: Lindsey Lowe
Children's Publisher: Anne O'Daly

Photographic Credits:
Front Cover: Shutterstock (inset); Klaus Arras (main)
Back Cover: Klaus Arras
Alamy: Douglas Peebles Photography 7; **Corbis:** Morton Beebe 20; **Dorling Kindersley:** 6; **Fotolia:** 3, 19, 34; **istock:** 4, 5, 9, 10, 28, 31; **Shutterstock:** 1, 3, 5, 7, 8, 12, 13, 14, 15, 17, 23, 25, 30, 31, 32, 33, 35, 36, 38, 39.

With thanks to models:
Caspar, Eugene, Jeremy, Hannah

Cooking Editor
Angelika Ilies has always been interested in cookery and other countries. She studied nutritional sciences in college. She has lived in the United States, England, and Germany. She has also traveled extensively and collected international recipes on her journeys. Angelika has written more than 70 cookbooks and cooking card series. She currently lives in Frankfurt, Germany, with her two children and has spent much time researching children's nutrition. Both children regularly cook with their mother.

Contents

A trip around
MEXICO

Mexico is the United States' southern neighbor. It is a republic of thirty-one states and one federal district. Its northern border is partly formed by the Rio Grande. This river separates Mexico from the U.S. states New Mexico and Texas. Mexico is about three times the size of Texas. It forms a bent wedge between the Pacific Ocean and the Gulf of Mexico. To the south, its neighbors are Guatemala and Belize.

The climate in Mexico is varied, with wet and dry seasons in many parts of the country. Hurricanes sometimes batter the coasts. Volcanic eruptions, earthquakes, and tsunamis (huge waves) can also be a threat. Mexico has a long history. It has been home to several great civilizations. The last of these was the Aztec Empire, which was overthrown by Spain in 1521.

The North

The large Chihuahua Desert stretches across the border with the United States. It is enclosed between the Sierre Madre Oriental and the Sierra Madre Occidental. These great mountain ranges sweep southward through Mexico. They are separated by a central highland, known as the Altiplano Central. In the far west of Mexico, the Baja Peninsula juts into the Pacific Ocean. This peninsula is 775 miles long. It is

△ **Most Mexicans** are "mestizo"—they are of mixed Native American and Spanish blood. Spanish is the official language. Some people speak Mayan and other Mexican languages.

Contents

let's START COOKING

Cooking is fun—you learn about different ingredients and cooking methods, you find out how things taste, and you can serve a meal to your family and friends that you have cooked yourself! Some of the recipes in this book have steps that need adult help—ask a parent or other adult if they will be your kitchen assistant while you cook a meal.

This line tells you how many people the meal will feed.

In this box, you find out which ingredients you need for your meal.

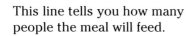

WHAT YOU NEED:

SERVES 4 PEOPLE:

2¼ cups white rice
4 eggs, beaten
light soy sauce
4 tablespoons
   groundnut
   or soy oil
2 green onions
⅓ cup peeled shrimps
⅓ cup ham
⅓ cup green peas

Check before you start that you have everything at home. If something is missing, write it on your shopping list. Get all the ingredients ready before you start cooking.

◁ Cooking is great fun and healthier than takeout food. I wonder what I should cook for dinner tonight? Tamales? Or tortillas with beef sauce?

! WHEN TO GET help

Most cooking involves cutting ingredients and heating them in some way, whether frying, boiling, or cooking in the oven. Each time you see this exclamation mark, be extra careful as you cook and make sure your adult kitchen assistant is around to help.

For many meals you need to chop an onion. First cut off a thin slice at both ends. Pull off the peel. Cut the onion in half from end to end. Put one half with the cut side down on the chopping board. Hold it with one hand and cut end-to-end slices with the other hand. Hold the slices together and cut across the slices to make small cubes. Make sure you do not cut yourself!

Other recipes in this book use fresh chilies. Always wear rubber or surgical gloves when chopping chilies. If you don't have any gloves, wash your hands very thoroughly afterward, and do not touch your skin for a while. Chili seeds and the white pith contain a substance that makes your skin burn. Trim off the stalk and halve the chili lengthways. Scrape out the seeds and throw them away.

A tortilladora is useful when you make a lot of tortillas. Line the base with plastic wrap. Place a ball of tortilla dough on top and close the press to make a tortilla.

Pestles and mortars help you grind herbs and spices. Put them in the bowl (the mortar), then push them against the sides with the stick (the pestle).

Colorful **Mexican pottery** dishes are great for serving salsas with a meal. Larger bowls can be used for rice.

A molinillo is an ancient tool for stirring and frothing Mexican chocolate drinks. You can use an ordinary whisk instead.

A trip around
MEXICO

Mexico is the United States' southern neighbor. It is a republic of thirty-one states and one federal district. Its northern border is partly formed by the Rio Grande. This river separates Mexico from the U.S. states New Mexico and Texas. Mexico is about three times the size of Texas. It forms a bent wedge between the Pacific Ocean and the Gulf of Mexico. To the south, its neighbors are Guatemala and Belize.

The climate in Mexico is varied, with wet and dry seasons in many parts of the country. Hurricanes sometimes batter the coasts. Volcanic eruptions, earthquakes, and tsunamis (huge waves) can also be a threat. Mexico has a long history. It has been home to several great civilizations. The last of these was the Aztec Empire, which was overthrown by Spain in 1521.

The North

The large Chihuahua Desert stretches across the border with the United States. It is enclosed between the Sierre Madre Oriental and the Sierra Madre Occidental. These great mountain ranges sweep southward through Mexico. They are separated by a central highland, known as the Altiplano Central. In the far west of Mexico, the Baja Peninsula juts into the Pacific Ocean. This peninsula is 775 miles long. It is

△ *Most Mexicans* are "mestizo"—they are of mixed Native American and Spanish blood. Spanish is the official language. Some people speak Mayan and other Mexican languages.

1

◁ **The North-West** of Mexico is mainly desert country—dry, barren, and dotted with cacti. Baja California is a long peninsula. It forms the Gulf of California.

NORTH AMERICA

MEXICO

SOUTH AMERICA

◁ **Mexico** is a Central American country. Its northern neighbor is the United States. In the south are Belize and Guatemala. It is about a fifth the size of the U.S.

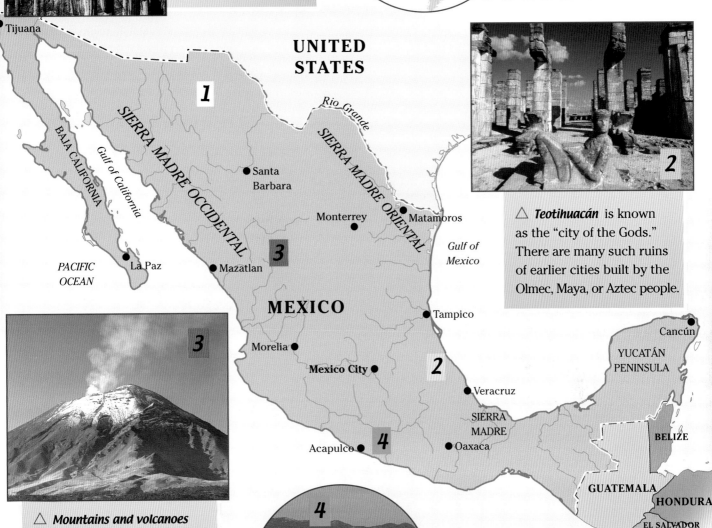

Tijuana

UNITED STATES

Rio Grande

BAJA CALIFORNIA

SIERRA MADRE OCCIDENTAL

Gulf of California

1

Santa Barbara

Monterrey

SIERRA MADRE ORIENTAL

Matamoros

Gulf of Mexico

PACIFIC OCEAN

La Paz

Mazatlan

3

Tampico

2

△ **Teotihuacán** is known as the "city of the Gods." There are many such ruins of earlier cities built by the Olmec, Maya, or Aztec people.

Cancún

YUCATÁN PENINSULA

MEXICO

Morelia

Mexico City

2

Veracruz

SIERRA MADRE

Acapulco

4

Oaxaca

BELIZE

GUATEMALA

HONDURA

EL SALVADOR

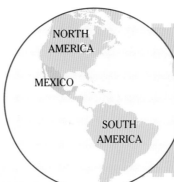

3

△ **Mountains and volcanoes** dominate much of Mexico. The Sierra Madre (mountains) follow the coastlines. Three major volcanoes—Pico de Orizaba, Popocatépetl, and Iztaccihuatl are covered in ice.

4

◁ **Acapulco** is a famous Mexican resort. It has beautiful scenery, great beaches, lots of watersports, bars, and restaurants. Other beach resorts are Cancún and Mazatlan.

covered by mountains and hot dry desert. Tijuana, its main city, calls itself "the gateway to Mexico." In the east and west narrow plains stretch along Mexico's coastlines. Here the climate is warm and humid.

Yucatán peninsula

A large corner of Mexico is called the Yucatán peninsula. It swings upward into the Gulf of Mexico and separates it from the Caribbean Sea. In the lowlands, rainwater and underground rivers have washed away the limestone rock.

They form tunnels and collapsed caverns, known as sinkholes or *cenotes*. Tourists come here to visit the ancient pyramids built by the Mayan people, who have lived and farmed in this area for more than 1,500 years. Many

▽ **El Castillo** is the grandest of the pyramids at Chichen Itza on the Yucatán peninsula. The temple of the Mayan god Kukulcan sits on top of the step pyramid. Twice a year, the sun casts a shadow in the shape of a plumed serpent, the symbol of this god.

Mayans still live in the region today. The huge Chicxulub crater is another famous landmark. Scientists believe that it was created when a giant asteroid crashed into Earth from Space.

Central Mexico

Much of Mexico's food is grown in the central plain. The highlands have pleasant weather, with springlike temperatures all year round. The capital is Mexico City, one of the world's largest cities. The city sits in a basin located 7,400 feet high on the central plateau. It is surrounded by mountains, and the air above the city traps the pollution from cars and factories. The polluted air hangs like a heavy blanket above the great city.

The Popocatépetl volcano is only 45 miles away from Mexico City. Its name is the Aztec word for "smoking mountain." The volcano continues to erupt. In 2007, "Popo" sent a plume of smoke 25,000 feet high in the air.

The South

In the southwestern states, mountains are covered with forests of pine and oak. The forests belong to groups of Native Americans who have long lived and worked in these remote mountains and deep valleys.

Along its border with Guatemala, Mexico has stretches of rainforest. But many trees are being cut to clear land for cattle-ranching and farming. This logging destroys the surroundings that forest birds, animals, and plants need to survive.

The state of Oaxaca has mountains, fast-flowing rivers, waterfalls, canyons, lagoons, and coastal plains. Some rivers are dammed to make electricity and to water the land.

△ *Mexico City* is Mexico's capital and its main place for business and culture. The ruins of five Aztec pyramids and the country's largest cathedral stand here. The old town center is a World Heritage site.

The food we grow in
MEXICO

Mexico produces plenty of fruit and vegetables, and its own staple—corn. The people rear cattle and catch fish.

C orn and chocolate are among the foods Mexico has given to the rest of the world. The country's varied landscape and climate allows a wide variety of plants to flourish. Native Americans farmed a wild grass called *teosinte*. They developed it into corn with plump kernels. Spanish explorers conquered the Aztec Empire in the sixteenth century. The Aztec people mixed dark, bitter chocolate with honey, seeds, and spices to make drinks. When the Spanish ships went back to Europe, they took all interesting seeds with them, including cocoa (chocolate) beans.

Cattle country

The Spanish conquerors first brought cattle, pigs, and horses to Mexico. The country has plenty of open grassland for herds of cattle to graze on. Today, Mexico produces and exports large amounts of beef, and Mexicans eat many beef dishes. *Machacado* is a type of shredded dried beef, popular in the north. It is often served with onions, tomatoes, and chili peppers. The northern city of Chihuahua is an important center for milk and cheese.

▽ **Spanish cattle** graze on the sparse, dry grasslands in the northwest of the country. Mexican cowboys test their skills in rodeos, called *charreadas*. They compete under strict rules.

CHILI-ING FACTS!

There are more than are 200 types of chilies in the world. Most come from Mexico. They vary in shape, color, and heat. The hottest are called habanero.

Animals are reared on the northern plain near the Gulf of Mexico. Farmers also grow large amounts of corn, wheat, oats, potatoes, beans, nuts, and apples in the north.

Small farms

In central Mexico, farmers grow foods like corn, wheat, squash, peanuts, chilies, vegetables, and beans on small plots of land. They still use traditional farming methods. People buy and sell produce at colorful markets. These range from neighborhood street stalls to Mexico City's huge La Merced, a market that stretches along several blocks.

Southern states

The Gulf Coast and the south of Mexico have a tropical climate—it is always hot and humid. Here people grow bananas, coconuts, papaya, pineapple, and mangoes. Scented vanilla pods from a type of Mexican orchid, sugarcane, coffee, and cocoa beans are also important crops from the south. Farmers in the Oaxaca

region also grow corn, beans, sugarcane, citrus fruit, and melons. The people of lowland Yucatán cultivate rice, wheat, squash, chilis, and tomatoes. They keep cows and pigs. Beekeepers here produce delicious honey.

△ *Tropical fruits* like mangoes (above), bananas, and pineapples grow well in the hot and humid south of the country.
▽ *Cacti are grown* on small farms in dry and highland areas. Cactus fruit, known as prickly pears, are a popular snack.

Fishing grounds

The waters off Mexico's long coastlines on the Gulf of Mexico and the Pacific Ocean are full of fish and seafood. The Baja peninsula also has many miles of coast. Fishers catch lobster, shark, tuna, sardines, mackerel, and many other kinds of fish and shellfish.

Here and on the coast of the Yucatán peninsula, tanks of seawater are left outside to dry. The seawater is burned off by the sun, and salt flakes appear. These are cleaned for use in cooking and cleaning materials. Shrimps, sea bass, and shark are caught in the seas off Yucatán. Visiting anglers come to catch tuna, marlin, and sailfish. Laws regulate the sport and stop overfishing.

◁ **Fishing boats** set out from many coastal ports to catch snapper, mackerel, mullet, and shrimps in the Gulf of Mexico, and lobster, anchovies, and skipjack tuna in the Pacific Ocean. The fish is then sold fresh at Mexico's many markets.

CORN CONQUERS THE WORLD

Native American people have grown Indian corn for about 7,000 years. The Mayans of southern Mexico and the Yucatán once believed that their gods made people out of cornmeal. From Mexico the use of corn spread north to the United States and south to Peru. It is now the most widely grown staple food in the entire world.

let's make...
TASTY TORTILLAS

My friends and I love tortillas. You can buy them ready-made but they're so easy to make that we always cook our own. Once you know how to do it, you can create all the different styles.

WHAT YOU NEED:

MAKES 12 TORTILLAS:

2 cups masa harina
a pinch of salt
about 1½ cups hot water
1 teaspoon shortening

◁ My favorite tortilla filling is ground beef *(see pages 16–17)*. But you can make lots of other things with tortillas, too. Try Eggs Ranchero, for example *(see pages 40–41)*.

WHAT'S THIS: *masa harina?*

Masa harina is a flour made from corn, but don't confuse it with cornmeal! You can buy it in Mexican stores.

MY TIP

If the wrap sticks, it means that your dough is too wet. Scrape it off, add a little more masa harina, knead, and try again.

1 Put the masa harina and salt into a large bowl. Put the water into a saucepan, and bring it to a boil. Pour the water over the masa harina. Put the shortening into a skillet, turn the heat to medium, and simmer gently until it is melted. Pour it into the bowl. **!**

2 Combine everything with a big spoon—but be careful: it's very hot! Set the bowl to one side and allow to cool for a few minutes so you can touch the dough. **!**

3 Knead the dough with both hands to mix everything together, until it becomes a big, doughy ball.

4 Divide the dough into twelve smaller portions. This is easy: first halve the ball, then halve each smaller ball again. Next, divide each of these four portions into three balls. Allow the balls to rest for about 1 hour.

5 Take one dough ball at a time and place it between two layers of plastic wrap. Roll a rolling pin over it, until you get a circle of about 6–7 inches across. Gently pull off the wrap (see My Tip on the left).

6 Heat the skillet. Put in one tortilla at a time and cook for 1 minute. Turn it over with a spatula and cook the other side for 1 minute. Cover the cooked tortillas with a clean kitchen cloth to keep them warm until all are cooked. **!**

let's make...
BEEF SAUCE

This ground beef sauce is great—you can eat it wrapped in tortillas, piled into taco shells, with boiled rice or noodles, or as a filling for a potato jacket.

▽ This ground beef recipe is my Mom's, and she learned it from her Mom. She says the secret is in the spices, but she doesn't mean adding lots of chilies!

WHAT YOU NEED:

SERVES 4 PEOPLE:

1 large onion
1 garlic clove
2 small red chilies
1 can (14 oz) red kidney beans
2 tablespoons oil
½ lb ground beef

1 large can
  peeled and
  chopped tomatoes
salt and pepper
½ teaspoon ground cumin
½ teaspoon fresh thyme leaves

PLUS GARNISHES:

shredded
lettuce
grated cheese
diced tomato
chopped
onion
sliced olives

WHAT SORT OF chili?

There are hundreds of different chilies. Some are very mild, others are devilishly hot. If you don't know what a chili will taste like, use only a very small amount. Read more about using chilies on page 5.

1 Peel the onion, then chop it into small cubes *(see page 5)*. Wash the chilies. Cut off the stems. **!**

2 With a knife, slit the chilies open and deseed them *(see page 5)*. Wash the thyme. Pull the leaves off the stems, then chop them. **!**

3 Open the can of kidney beans. Place a sieve over a bowl, and tip the contents of the can into the sieve. Pour over some cold water from the faucet to wash the beans, then let them drip and drain in the sieve.

4 Heat the oil in a large saucepan. Add the chopped onion and fry over medium heat for about 5 minutes, until it is transparent (see-through). Stir the onion from time to time with a wooden spoon so it does not burn. **!**

6 Add the chilies, drained kidney beans, and canned tomatoes. Squash the tomatoes with the back of the spoon. Season with salt, pepper, cumin, and thyme. Stir everything to mix it well. Turn the heat to low and simmer the sauce gently for about 30 minutes; stir from time to time. Serve with tortillas and the garnishes.

5 Add the ground beef to the pan. Squash the beef with the back of your spoon and fry it, stirring, until it no longer looks pink and turns brown.

let's make...
GUACAMOLE

Guacamole is a delicious, no-cook, smooth avocado purée. We eat it as a dipping sauce, or salsa. And we also pile it into tortillas together with other sauces, cheese, or sour cream!

WHAT YOU NEED:

SERVES 4 PEOPLE:

2 firm tomatoes
1 small onion
1 small red chili
2–3 ripe avocados
4–5 tablespoons lime juice
a pinch of salt
1 handful of
      fresh cilantro

◁ Instead of dipping tortilla chips, why not try celery or carrot sticks, strips of crunchy bell peppers, or pieces of cauliflower?

MY TIP

If you use only half an avocado, the flesh turns brown very fast, and that doesn't look terribly appetizing. Squirt some fresh lemon or lime juice all over the avocado flesh—and it'll stay a nice yellowish green.

1 Wash the tomatoes. Halve them and cut out the stem. With a spoon, scrape out the seeds. Chop the tomato flesh into small cubes. Peel and chop the onion *(see page 5)*. Wash and chop the chili *(see page 5)*.

2 Halve the avocados lengthways, cutting down to the pit. Twist the halves against each other so they come apart. Jab the knife into the pit. Turn the knife to pull out the pit.

3 With a spoon, scrape the avocado flesh out of the shells and put it in a blender. Add the lime juice and purée both. Stir the tomato, onion, and chili into the purée. Stir in a pinch of salt to season.

4 Wash the cilantro. Shake it dry, then pat the leaves dry with some paper towels. Pull the leaves off the stems and chop them with a knife. Stir the chopped cilantro into the purée, or sprinkle the leaves over the top.

MAKE YOUR OWN CHIPS

Pile a few freshly made tortillas on top of each other, then cut them into wedges. Spread out the wedges on a baking tray and leave them to dry for 30 minutes. Heat the oven to 350°F. Place the wedges on a wire rack and bake them for 15 minutes until they are crisp and curl a little.

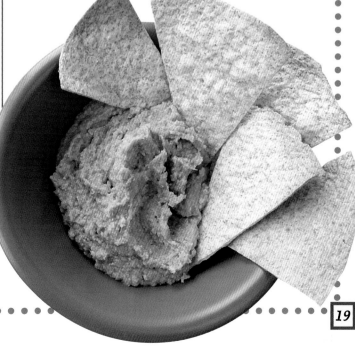

How we celebrate in
MEXICO

Mexicans love to celebrate. There are many national festivals. Some, such as Independence Day or Cinco de Mayo, celebrate a day in the country's history. Others, such as Three Kings or Easter, are religious holidays. Aside from the national festivals, there are also many village celebrations. Often these festivities honor the patron saint of a village.

Independence Day

The biggest national event is Independence Day, known as *fiestas patrias*. It is celebrated over two days every year, on September 15 and 16. It all started in 1810. A priest, Father Hidalgo, rang the church bells in the town of Dolores. He asked the people to take up arms against the Spanish who had ruled Mexico for nearly 300 years.

Today Mexicans all over the world celebrate this event. They decorate their houses with flags, and on the evening of September 15, they enjoy food and drinks with family and friends. Then they gather in the main squares of towns and villages. In Mexico City, a bell is rung, and the president and the people shout, "Long live Mexico!" They wave Mexican flags, light huge fireworks, and dance until late into the night. There are rodeos, parades, bullfights, and horse shows. The next day, everyone goes to watch more parades.

AMAZING MAZATLÁN

About 400,000 revelers from Mexico and other countries celebrate the carnival in Mazatlán. It is the third largest carnival after those in New Orleans and Rio.

▽ *Carnival* is the festival before Lent. People dance in the streets, and there are costume parades and fantastic fireworks.

Day of the Dead

For this Mexican festival, on November 1 and 2, lots of skulls and skeletons are on display. This may seem a bit sad. But it is, in fact, a festive occasion. Families honor and remember their dead. They gather at the graves of family members and decorate the plots with flowers. They enjoy specially prepared foods together with relatives, and tell stories of the departed. The souls of the dead, they believe, are all around them.

People also bake a special bread for the day, called the Bread of the Dead, or *pan de muerto*. They add a small skeleton to the dough and the person who bites on this skeleton is said to be very lucky in the coming year.

▽ *Flowers, fruit, and items* that remind people of their dead are set up on an altar at home. This may include a favorite book or a musical instrument or some other pet object of the dead person.

Three Kings

Three Kings' Day, or Epiphany, is celebrated on January 6. The festival remembers the three kings, Gaspar, Melchior, and Baltazar. According to the Bible, they offered their gifts to the newborn Jesus.

Now Three Kings is the day when Mexican children receive most of their presents, rather than at Christmas. A special sweet cake, called *rosca de reyes*, is baked. It contains a figurine of the baby Jesus. According to tradition, the person who finds it has to give a party on February 2, Candlemas Day, and serve *tamales*.

Semana Santa

Semana Santa, or Holy Week, is the week before Easter. All over the country, people celebrate the last days of the life of Christ. Costumed people perform the Passion of Christ. Easter itself is a quiet festival. Traditionally there are no Easter eggs or chocolate bunnies.

△ **The Last Supper** is one of the stages in the Life of Christ. Pictures, like this sand sculpture, are made all over the country. People also act out the Bible story.

EASTER WITH A BANG

As part of Easter and Holy Week celebrations, people used to explode sculptures of Judas. This is because Judas betrayed Jesus. However, some explosions got a little out of hand. So the government banned this custom.

let's make...
KINGS' CAKE

This cake is called *rosca de reyes*. We eat it on January 6. The cake usually has a little baby figurine baked into it—this is meant to be the baby Jesus hiding from King Herod.

WHAT YOU NEED:

MAKES 1 CAKE:

4 cups all-purpose flour
1 tablespoon fresh yeast
3 tablespoons superfine sugar
½ cup lukewarm milk
½ cup softened butter
a pinch of salt
grated zest of 1 organic orange
grated zest of ½ organic lemon

3 medium eggs
4 ounces mixed candied fruits, plus more for decorating the cake
butter for greasing the tray

PLUS:

a baby doll or any other small soft toy

◁ Last year I got the slice of cake with the baby Jesus in it! Now I am going to start a collection of figurines.

I CAN'T GET *fresh yeast!*

Instead of 1 tablespoon fresh yeast, you can use ½ tablespoon active dried yeast. You can buy it in a packet. Put this into 1 cup lukewarm water and wait for a few minutes for it to turn liquid.

1 Place a fine sieve over a large bowl. Tip in the flour and shake it gently so it falls into the bowl. This will make the flour extra-fine. With a spoon, make a hollow in the center of the flour heap.

3 After 20 minutes, add the rest of the sugar, the softened butter, salt, and grated orange and lemon zests to the bowl. Mix everything together with your hands and knead until it becomes a smooth dough.

2 Crumble the yeast into a cup. Add 1 tablespoon sugar and the milk and stir. Pour the yeast mixture into the hollow in the flour. Sprinkle a little flour over the top. Cover the bowl with a clean cloth and allow it to stand in a warm place for 20 minutes.

4 Chop the candied fruits and stir them into the dough. Put the baby Jesus or other toy into the dough now. Shape the dough into a thick ring. Put a little butter on some paper towels and rub this over a baking tray to grease it. Place the ring on the tray. Cover it with a cloth and stand it in a warm place for about 30 minutes.

5 Heat the oven to 350°F. Crack the egg and separate out the egg yolk. Stir it with a fork until it is all smooth. Brush the cake with the egg yolk. Gently press pieces of candied fruit into the dough for decoration. Bake the cake for 30 minutes, until it is golden brown. Put on oven mitts, take out the cake, and place it on a rack to cool.

let's make...
TAMALES

Whoever finds the baby Jesus in their kings' cake on January 6 has to invite all their friends to share tamales on the *día de la candelaria*! It's always on February 2.

WHAT YOU NEED:

SERVES 4 PEOPLE:

dried corn husks or banana
   leaves
4 cups masa harina
1 cup chicken stock
salt and black pepper
3 ounces shortening
2–3 chilies
1 lb chicken breast, boned
   and skinned
1 onion
2 tablespoons oil
2 garlic cloves
1 small can tomatoes
   (14 ounces)
ground cumin
1 handful fresh cilantro

◁ Dad likes his tamales with
a fiery hot chili sauce. I prefer
a milder salsa. They are also
delicious with yogurt.

HOW DO I USE <u>corn husks?</u>

Before you start cooking, put the corn husks or banana leaves into a bowl filled with warm water. Soak them for 1–2 hours to make them soft. If you cannot get any leaves, use aluminum foil instead; don't soak the foil.

1 Put the masa harina in a bowl, add the stock and salt, and stir together until it is a thick mixture. Melt the shortening in a skillet. Stir it into the mixture. Once it has cooled enough, knead with your hands. Cover with a clean cloth and set it aside.

2 Wash, trim, and deseed the chilies *(see page 5)*. Wash the chicken, pat it dry, and cut it into very small cubes. Peel and chop the onion *(see page 5)*. Wash the cilantro and shake it dry. Chop the leaves.

3 Put the oil into a large saucepan and set it on medium heat. Add the onion and fry for 5 minutes until it is golden. Add the chicken and fry for 5 minutes until it is brown all over. Stir with a spoon so it doesn't burn.

4 Peel the garlic and press it into the saucepan. Stir in the chilies and tomatoes. Squash tomatoes with a spoon. Add salt, cumin, and pepper. Cook for a few minutes. Stir in cilantro.

5 Spread out the corn leaves. Place 1½ tablespoons of corn dough on each leaf. Spread it out with the back of a spoon. Put 1½ tablespoons of the chicken filling on top. Close the dough over the chicken, then close the leaves over the dough parcel (roll it up one way, then turn up the sides). Fill a large saucepan 2–3 inches deep with water and bring to a boil.

6 Line a steam basket with leaves. Cram in the tamales. Place the basket in the saucepan and cover. Cook for 1 hour over low heat. The tamales are done when the leaves come off easily.

How we celebrate at home in
MEXICO

A side from the large national festivals, Mexican families celebrate religious feast days and family events. For most events, people sing, dance, and have festive meals. Houses are decorated in bright colors.

The posadas

The lead-up to Christmas is an important time for the family to get together. In the days before December 25, children go from house to house in a procession known as *la posada*. The two children at the front carry a model of the stable with the manger. The figures show Joseph, Maria, and the baby Jesus. The children also carry long, lit candles.

At each house, the children ask if they may come in. At first they are not allowed to enter. After some more songs, they will be invited into the house. Then everyone prays together. The posada usually finishes with a *piñata*, just like for a birthday party *(see pages 32–33)*.

On Christmas Eve, there are fireworks at midnight to announce the birth of Christ. Families go to midnight mass. Afterward, they celebrate in their own homes with a great feast. The food varies from region to region, but tamales are often a part of it.

Christmas Day itself is a quiet day in Mexico, and people don't normally exchange presents until the Day of the Kings.

Weddings

Mexican weddings are large events, with many guests. The guests are known as *madrinas* (godmothers) and *padrinos* (godfathers). They all have a special role to fulfill. Two of the guests, the flower girl and the ring bearer, are dressed as miniature versions of the marrying couple.

A close friend of the couple may place a rosary or a chain of twisted orange blossoms in a figure-eight around the couple. This symbolizes that they are bound together.

After the church ceremony, there is a big *fiesta*. A mariachi band plays festive music and the newlyweds open the dance. These bands plays Latin music, with salsa, merengue, and flamenco dance rhythms. Traditional food is served, usually including tortillas, tamales, spicy rice, chicken, and beef dishes.

◁ **Papel picado** are sheets of colored paper that are cut out to make a pattern, for example, flowers. Papel picado are hung up for birthdays, local festivals, or for decoration.

Birthdays

Mexican children are lucky—they have two "birthdays." The first one is the annual return of the day on which they were born. The second is their name or saint's day. This is the calendar day of the saint after whom they were named, such as José or Teresa. On their saint's day, children go to church and get blessed by the priest.

Birthday parties always include a *piñata*. This is a large papier mâché animal in bright colors that is filled with candies or gifts. It hangs from a tree. One child is blindfolded. The child is given a stick, turned around a few times, and then he or she has to bash the piñata three times. As the piñata bursts, everyone runs to grab their share of gifts.

The quinceaños

Quinceaños means "fifteen years," and this is a special birthday for girls in Mexico. The day marks the fact that the young girl has become a woman. It is a Catholic celebration, and starts with a thanksgiving mass at church. Traditionally, the young woman wears a pink dress and a tiara because she is considered a "princess" for that day. There is always a big party afterward. The girl dances the first dance, which is a waltz, with her dad.

▽ **Mariachi** are bands of Mexican musicians who play at weddings and on Mother's Day. They play various instruments, including violins, trumpets, and Spanish guitars. Often they wear special costumes.

Religious ceremonies

Mexico is a Christian country, and the vast majority of Mexicans are Catholics. Many family celebrations follow the customs of the Catholic Church. After birth, children are baptized. When they are aged eight or nine, they will go to communion. Later, young adults will get married in church. They will go to church regularly, and observe the church's funeral rites when someone dies.

In some rural areas, however, the old Mayan and Aztec customs have also survived. In the days of the Mayan empire, shamans were priests. Today, there are still shamans but most now work as healers.

▽ **A bride** wears a white wedding dress and a veil. She says her vows in church, before a priest. Afterward there is a big party for family and friends to celebrate.

△ **On Ash Wednesday**, after the carnival celebrations, people go to church to confess their sins. The priest places an ashen cross on each churchgoer's forehead. This is the start of Lent, when the fasting begins.

let's make a...
PIÑATA

Our favorite birthday game is hitting a piñata until it bursts and spills all the candies inside. It takes a few days to make one, so don't leave it to the last minute.

WHAT YOU NEED:

MAKES 1 PIÑATA:

one or more large
round balloons
lots of old
newspapers
school glue
scissors or craft
knife
tape
piñata patterns for
the head and
legs
thin cardboard
colored tissue paper

FOR THE FILLING:

candies of your choice

◁ Hang the piñata from a tree or a wash line. Each child gets three hits. Take turns to be fair and stand back from the swinger!

WHAT KIND OF _patterns?_

You can find piñata patterns in the stores. Bulls and donkeys are common shapes, but you can also make your own. Try a moon shape, or a house, for example. Or make your favorite cartoon character.

1 Tear the newspaper into long strips, about 1 inch by 5 inches. Pour the glue into an old bowl (ask your Mom!) and put the paper strips in the glue to soak. Blow up the balloon and tie it with a knot.

2 Cover the balloon all over with the gluey paper. Allow the paper to dry. Repeat this two or three more times. Allow to dry each time.

3 **!** With a knife or scissors, cut a lid into the side of the newspaper shape—ask for help. It will pop the balloon. Cut out head and leg patterns. Place them on thin cardboard. Draw around the outline, then cut out the cardboard. Follow the instructions that come with the piñata pattern. Tape the head and legs to the balloon.

4 Cut the colored tissue paper into strips, about 1 inch by 2 inches. Glue one end of each strip to the piñata and leave the other end to hang loose. In the next row, overlap the strips as in a row of roof tiles.

5 Fill the body of the piñata with goodies—candies, toys, money, lots of small things. Tape the lid that you cut out earlier back in place.

6 To play the game, blindfold the first player. Turn him or her around a few times and give them a stick. Point them in the right direction so they don't hit you! Each one is allowed to hit the piñata three times. When it breaks, share all the goodies.

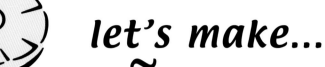

let's make...
PIÑA COLADA

Lots of fruits are grown in Mexico, from strawberries to mangoes. Most people love refreshing fruit drinks. One of the favorites is this **alcohol-free** cocktail.

WHAT YOU NEED:

MAKES 4-6 COCKTAILS:

1 small fresh pineapple
1 cup sweetened coconut cream
1 cup cold milk
lots of crushed ice

DECORATIONS:

pineapple slices
maraschino cherries
cocktail umbrellas
long straws

◁ If you don't like creamy drinks, use water instead of milk. It makes a lighter drink.

MAKING _crushed ice_ !

The easiest way is to use an ice crusher. Just fill it with ice cubes and turn the handle to crush the ice. If you don't have an ice crusher, put the ice cubes in a ziptop bag and pound them with a hammer or mallet.

1 Peel the pineapple. Chop off the green leaves at the top and a slice from the bottom so the pineapple can stand up by itself.

!

2 Slice down the sides of the pineapple to cut off the peel. Now cut the pineapple into fourths from the top down. Cut out the hard center and throw it away (*see My Tip below*).

!

3 Set some pineapple chunks aside for the garnish. Put the rest into a blender or purée them with a hand-held blender until it is a smooth liquid.

!

4 Put the coconut cream and the milk into a clean bowl or cup. Use the hand-held blender to mix them well together and make them foam a little.

5 Stir the pineapple purée into the coconut milk mix. Fill some tall glasses with crushed ice. Pour the cocktail over the ice. Garnish the drinks with pineapple chunks and maraschino cherries and decorate each glass with a cocktail umbrella.

VARIATION

BERRY COLADA: Purée 3 cups mixed frozen berries with 1 cup pineapple juice and 1 cup coconut cream in the blender, then pour over crushed ice as above.

MY TIP

If you find fresh pineapple slices or chunks in your superstore, you can use these and save time and trouble peeling a whole pineapple.

How we live in
MEXICO

People in Mexico have large families. There can be as many as ten people in one household. Many mothers stay at home to look after the children. Some fathers have to find work far away from their families. Sometimes they work in other countries, for example in the United States. Children often have to help with the household chores.

Most Mexicans are *mestizos*. That means, there were Spanish and Native American people in their family in the past. Children have first names followed by the surname of the father and the mother's maiden name.

City life

In Mexico City, many people work in offices. Many homes are as comfortable as those of people who live in cities elsewhere. The children go to schools and use the latest textbooks and equipment. A network of buses carries people to work and school. Buses link the city with the rest of the country. Mexico City also has a modern subway system.

The busy streets are lined with stalls selling snacks, fruit, and flowers. But the streets are also "home" for some of Mexico's poorest children. These street children are left to fend for themselves because their parents have died, or because the children have been left, or because they have learning difficulties.

▽ **This small church** on the Yucatán peninsula is covered in Mexican flags. Religion plays a major role in many people's life. Almost half of Mexicans worship at church at least once a week.

Village life

As in the cities, there is also a large gap between the lives of the rich and the poor in the country. In some Native American villages people still live simple lives. Their houses are made of adobe—a mixture of mud, straw, and water—and the roofs are made of thatch. Most of their meals consist of corn, beans, squash, and chili peppers grown in local fields. These foods form the basis of the Mexican diet everywhere. In richer areas people can also afford to eat meat and fish.

Life at school

Young children have to attend preschool from the ages of three to six. At elementary school, the school day is only about four hours long. There are two sessions. Some children attend school in the morning, while older ones go to school in the afternoon. This shift system allows more children to get at least a basic education. Not all Mexican children go on to high school. In the country especially, children are often needed at home. They help their parents in the fields and look after younger brothers and sisters. Many children cannot go to school beyond sixth grade because they have to work and earn money.

The school day

Mexican people are very patriotic—they love their country. On Monday mornings in school, pupils raise the Mexican flag and sing their national anthem. The teachers may also give them a talk about good behavior. Children learn Spanish, math, history, science, and ethics. They also study geography and the environment. At recess they play outside and eat their snacks. They enjoy playground games, like jumping ropes and spinning tops.

Time off

Families in Mexico like to enjoy themselves. On weekends in the city they go to parks, museums, public buildings, and other

▽ *Transportation* is a great problem in the big cities. In Mexico City, the exhaust fumes choke the town. The government has asked people to observe a "day without a car" program at least twice a week, and to use buses, like these, whenever possible.

attractions. Mexican children go to the movies, and they also play soccer, baseball, or handball. A visit to a bullfight or a rodeo is another popular pastime. People get together for a chat over an ice cream or a cake in an outdoor bar or café. Mexicans are mostly Catholic and attend church regularly. On festival days, there are lively celebrations.

▽ **Street vendors** sell fresh fruit juices from tricycles or carts. People might buy a refreshing melon drink and sit in the shade for a chat with a friend.

Meal times

Mexican families start the day with sweet rolls for breakfast. Women usually prepare and cook the food. Eggs ranchero or thin cornmeal pancakes called tortillas are a popular lunch dish. The tortillas are often filled with mixtures of meat, vegetables, and cheese, and spiced with a dash of hot chili sauce. Sometimes they are baked in the oven to make enchiladas. Bean soups feature on many family menus and Mexican rice is a typical everyday meal. Burgers and fries are children's favorites, as anywhere.

let's make...
EGGS RANCHERO

In the mornings, everyone rushes around to get ready, but Mom says we must eat something hot before we leave. This egg and tortilla dish is one of our favorites.

◁ I use a heavy nonstick skillet. It allows me to use less butter or oil, or even leave the fat out altogether.

WHAT YOU NEED:

SERVES 4 PEOPLE:

1 cup tomato salsa (from the jar)
1 tablespoon butter or oil for frying
4 eggs
4 wheat or corn tortillas *(see pages 14–15)*
¼ cup grated cheese (for example Cheddar)
salt and pepper

FOR THE GARNISH:

a few leaves iceberg lettuce, shredded into small strips
1 tomato

ARE *eggs* HEALTHY?

Eggs are a good source of high-quality protein. They also provide vitamin A and other vitamins and minerals. They are high in cholesterol, but that is only a problem if people have a disorder and cannot process it.

1 Wash the lettuce leaves and shake them dry. Cut them into thin strips. Wash and dry the tomato. Cut it into slices.

!

2 Heat the salsa in a small saucepan, stirring from time to time. Heat each tortilla on a separate plate in the microwave for 1 minute. Spread the salsa over the hot tortillas.

!

3 Heat the butter or oil in a skillet over medium heat. Crack one egg into the pan and fry it until it is set. Lift it out with a spatula and place it on top of the salsa on a tortilla. Repeat with the other three eggs.

!

4 Preheat the oven to 350°F. Sprinkle the tortillas with grated cheese. Season with a little salt and pepper.

5 Put the plates with the tortillas in the oven for 5 minutes, or until the cheese has melted. Garnish with lettuce strips and tomato slices, and serve immediately.

MAKE YOUR OWN salsa

Heat 2 tablespoons oil in a skillet and cook 1 chopped onion and 1 crushed garlic clove for about 5 minutes, stirring from time to time. Stir in 1 can (14 ounces) chopped tomatoes, crumble in five dried chilies, and add ½ teaspoon salt. Cook for 10 minutes, then use in Step 2 above.

let's make...
BEAN SOUP

Have you ever tasted a homemade bean soup? There is nothing like it, I promise you! Forget about cans—this is the real thing. And it's good for you too.

WHAT YOU NEED:

SERVES 4 PEOPLE:

1½ cups canned black Mexican beans (or calypso beans or azuki beans)
1½ cups canned corn kernels
4 cups chicken or vegetable stock
2 green chilies
3 onions
2 garlic cloves
1 lb fresh tomatoes
4 tablespoons oil
salt and black pepper
2 tablespoons vinegar
1 teaspoon ground cumin
fresh cilantro leaves

◁ Some people use bacon drippings instead of oil to fry the onions in this recipe. The dripping gives the soup a delicious meaty flavor.

USING *dried beans*

Dried beans will give an even better flavor. Soak ½ cup dried beans in 1½ cups water for six hours. Cook the beans in a heavy metal saucepan for 1½ hours. Then continue with Step 2 of the recipe on the right.

1 Put the stock and the beans into a large saucepan. Heat for about 10 minutes over gentle heat.

2 Wash, trim, and deseed the chilies. Peel and chop the onions and the garlic *(see page 5)*.

3 Put all the tomatoes into a small bowl and pour over some boiling water. Leave them in the water for 1 minute. Take them out with tongs. Pull off the skin with a knife. Cut out the stem end and chop the flesh.

4 Heat the oil in a large saucepan. Add the chopped onion and garlic, and fry for 5 minutes, or until they are transparent (see-through). Add the chilies and the chopped tomatoes. Sprinkle in the salt, pepper, cumin, and vinegar. Stir everything well.

5 Ladle half the beans with their liquid into a blender and purée them. Return the puréed beans to the remaining beans. Add the onion mixture and stir well.

6 If the soup seems too thick, add a few tablespoons of cold water and stir well. Heat the soup over gentle heat. Check the seasoning. Sprinkle with cilantro leaves and serve immediately.

let's make...
MEXICAN RICE

We often eat a rice dish for our evening meal. It's a great way to use up leftovers, whether you have some peas or a bit of chicken from Sunday lunch. Beats burgers any time!

WHAT YOU NEED:

SERVES 4 PEOPLE:

4 lbs beef tomatoes
3 onions
5 garlic cloves
3 cups vegetable stock
1 tablespoon tomato purée
2 cups long-grain rice
2 carrots
1 green bell pepper
salt and pepper
fresh cilantro leaves

◁ Sometimes we chop in a bit of spicy fried sausage and some shrimps. The two are great companions—plus some garbanzos to make it perfect!

ALL ABOUT rice

Rice came to our country originally from Asia, some 4,000 years ago. It is now a staple part of our diet—that means, we eat it all the time, in soups, with main courses, and as a sweet and milky rice dish, too.

1 Make a cut in the top of each tomato. Place them in a bowl with boiling water for 1 minute. Lift them out. Pull off the skins with your fingers. Roughly chop the tomatoes.

2 Peel and roughly chop the onions and garlic cloves *(see page 5)*. Put the onion, garlic, and tomatoes into a blender. Mix everything to a smooth purée.

3 Put the stock into a large saucepan and stir in the tomato purée. Heat the mixture until it boils. Add the rice and stir. Bring to a boil again. Turn the heat to low, cover the saucepan, and gently cook the mixture for about 10 minutes.

4 Wash and scrape the carrots clean. Wash the bell pepper, halve it, and scrape out all the seeds. Cut the carrots and the pepper first into long strips, then into small cubes.

5 Add carrot and pepper cubes to the rice in the saucepan and stir to mix well. Cover with the lid and cook for another 10 minutes.

6 Check if everything is done. The vegetables should still be a little crunchy. Check the seasoning. Transfer the rice to a bowl, sprinkle with fresh cilantro leaves, and serve.

Look it up
MEXICO

avocado the fruit of a tree native to Mexico; it is peeled and the pit removed

carnival the festivities before Lent; usually in late February or early March

chili a small, hot fruit, available in different colors, shapes, and sizes, and varying in degrees of heat; needs to be treated carefully and used sparingly

guacamole a dip of mashed avocados, chilies, lemon or lime juice, onions, tomatoes, and spices

mariachi a traditional musical band that plays at weddings

masa harina a flour made from corn

Mestizos people of mixed European and Latin American origin

molinillo a traditional Mexican whisk or chocolate stirrer

papel picado colorful paper tissues that are punched with holes to form a pattern; used as colorful decorations at festivals

piñata a large, hollow papier mâché object containing candies and gifts

posadas the traditional celebrations in the last nine days before Christmas

quinceaños a girl's fifteenth birthday, when she is said to become a woman

rosca de reyes Kings' Cake, made for the Day of the Three Kings, or Epiphany; it contains a figurine of the baby Jesus

salsa any kind of sauce, but often a spicy tomato sauce

Semana Santa Holy Week, the week before Easter, a traditional time of reenacting the Passion of Christ

shamans originally Mayan sorcerers, today often traditional healers

tamales corn tortillas filled with meat and vegetables, then wrapped in corn husks and steamed

tortilla a flat, thin, round bread made from corn flour; the basis of many Mexican meals

Find out more
MEXICO

Books to read

Ainsworth-Olawsky, Lynn.
Colors of Mexico.
First Avenue Editions, 1997.

Fontes, Justine and Ron.
Mexico (A to Z). Children's Press, CT, 2004

Heinrichs, Ann.
Mexico, A True Book.
Danbury: Children's Press, 1997.

Johnson, Tony and Winter, Jeanette.
Day of the Dead. San Diego: Harcourt
Brace & Company, 1997.

Johnston, Tony. **My Mexico/México mío.**
Putnam Juvenile, 1999

Marx, David. **Mexico, Rookie
Read-About Geography.** Danbury:
Children's Press, 2000.

Milord, Susan. **Mexico:
40 Activities to Experience
Mexico Past &
Present.** Williamson
Publishing, 1999.

Web sites to check out

**www.kidskonnect.com/Mexico/
MexicoHome.html**
Facts about Mexico, festivals, cooking etc.

**www.kidsculturecenter.com/mexico/
mex_cult.htm**
Information on culture, products and
recipes from a number of countries,
including Mexico

**www.geographia.com/mexico/
mexicohistory.htm**
All about Mexico's history and culture

http://mexicanfood.about.com
A lot of information about Mexican food
and cooking, plus recipes

www.mexgrocer.com/mexcocina.html
An online store for Mexican food and
utensils, with recipes

**www.apples4theteacher.com/elibrary/
mexico-the-country.html**
An electronic talking book about Mexico

Index

MEXICO